TV **COOKS**

Michael Barry

COOKS

Crafty
Classics

Photographs by Philip Webb

Published by BBC Books,
an imprint of BBC Worldwide Publishing.
BBC Worldwide Limited, Woodlands,
80 Wood Lane, London W12 0TT.

The recipes in this book first appeared in the following:
Michael Barry's Food & Drink Cookbook
©Michael Barry 1991
Michael Barry's Radio Times Cookery Year
©Michael Barry 1994

This edition first published 1996
© Michael Barry 1996
The moral right of the author
has been asserted

ISBN 0 563 38795 5

Edited by Pam Mallender
Designed by DW Design
Photographs by Philip Webb
Styling by Helen Payne
Home Economist Jane Stevenson

Set in New Caledonia and Helvetica
Printed and bound in Belgium by Proost NV
Colour separations by Colour Origination Ltd, London
Cover printed by Proost NV

Cover and frontispiece: Vegetarian Cassoulet.

CONTENTS

RECIPE NOTES

Eggs are size 2.
Wash all fresh produce before preparation and peel as necessary.
Spoon measurements are level. Always use proper measuring spoons:
1 teaspoon = 5ml and 1 tablespoon = 15ml.
Never mix metric or imperial measures in one recipe. Stick to one or the other.

HANDY CONVERSION TABLE

Weight		Volume		Linear	
15g	½oz	30ml	1fl oz	5mm	¼in
25g	1oz	50ml	2fl oz	10mm/1cm	½in
40g	1½oz	100ml	3½fl oz	2cm	¾in
55g	2oz	125ml	4fl oz	2.5cm	1in
85g	3oz	150ml	5fl oz (¼ pint)	5cm	2in
115g	4oz	175ml	6fl oz	7.5cm	3in
140g	5oz	200ml	7fl oz (⅓ pint)	10cm	4in
175g	6oz	225ml	8fl oz	13cm	5in
200g	7oz	250ml	9fl oz	15cm	6in
225g	8oz	300ml	10fl oz (½ pint)	18cm	7in
250g	9oz	350ml	12fl oz	20cm	8in
280g	10oz	400ml	14fl oz	23cm	9in
350g	12oz	425ml	15fl oz (¾ pint)	25cm	10in
375g	13oz	450ml	16fl oz	28cm	11in
400g	14oz	500ml	18fl oz	30cm	12in
425g	15oz	600ml	20fl oz (1 pint)		
450g	1lb	700ml	1¼ pints	**Oven temperatures**	
550g	1¼lb	850ml	1½ pints	225F	110C	GAS ¼
750g	1lb 10oz	1 litre	1¾ pints	250F	120C	GAS ½
900g	2lb	1.2 litres	2 pints	275F	140C	GAS 1
1kg	2¼lb	1.3 litres	2¼ pints	300F	150C	GAS 2
1.3kg	3lb	1.4 litres	2½ pints	325F	160C	GAS 3
1.8kg	4lb	1.7 litres	3 pints	350F	180C	GAS 4
2.25kg	5lb	2 litres	3½ pints	375F	190C	GAS 5
		2.5 litres	4½ pints	400F	200C	GAS 6
				425F	220C	GAS 7
				450F	230C	GAS 8
				475F	240C	GAS 9

Ⓥ **Suitable for vegetarians**

Ⓕ **Low fat**

❋ **Suitable for freezing**

I really enjoy the recipes gathered in this collection because they include some of my absolute favourites collected over many years.

They vary quite a lot, from the old-fashioned British dishes such as Cullen skink to the more exotic such as Shrimp Gumbo from New Orleans, or Chicken Tikka from the North West Frontier provinces of India. Some have been the biggest favourites of all time on the *Food & Drink* programme. Perhaps the best examples of this are the Salmon en Croûte which was so successful that weeks after we broadcast it no dinner party was complete without it, and the Steak in Cream Sauce, extremely rich and an unfailing hit, especially with dedicated carnivores.

If it's puddings you're after, these are the real McCoy. My all-time favourite, Bread and Butter Pudding, I have made in a delicate way and there is nothing old-fashioned about its lightness or delicacy. The same is true of Raspberry Fool, that perfect summer dessert with the very silly name.

The book's got a few basic recipes as well to help with the preparation of dishes and some really useful notes on shopping and choosing vegetables, fruits, cheeses and herbs. The pleasures of crafty cooking are that it should be fun to shop for, easy to make and taste delicious. I do hope you find we have managed to live up to that reputation in this collection.

Michael Barry.

INGREDIENTS

Bay leaves

Fresh bay leaves are deep green, firm and shiny with a dull surface underneath and a distinct fragrance. They have a strong, spicy flavour. The leaves are from an ornamental evergreen tree that can be pruned like hedges to a desired shape.

Cheese

Goats' cheese: this cheese tends to be produced on a small scale. Its zesty tart flavour varies from fresh and soft, to dry and crumbly. Soft enough to spread when young, it matures to become almost chalky. June is a good time for British goats' milk cheese as goats can only really be milked after the spring and the cheeses are, therefore, at their freshest and newest at this time of year. They come in a variety of forms, both plain, snow-white and flavoured with herbs and spices.
Gruyère: a celebrated Swiss cheese made from unpasteurised cows' milk. It is pale yellow and very firm and close-textured with a sprinkling of small holes. It is sweet and nutty. At its best it has a slight glistening of moisture around the holes.
Emmental: one of the world's greatest cheeses this is named after the Emme valley, near Bern in Switzerland, where it originated. Famous for its large, round holes it is deep golden yellow with a firm, smooth texture. It is mellow and sweet with a lingering hint of hazelnuts. It is made from unpasteurised cows' milk and ripened for at least four months, often longer. Avoid any that has too many holes or shows any signs of cracking.

Dried pulses

Chick peas: pale golden and knobbly they have a wonderfully rich nutty flavour when cooked. They are the seed of a bush cultivated in southern Europe.
Haricot beans: these small, white, plump roundish beans cook to a melting tenderness.

Fromage frais

This is a very lightly fermented, soft, creamy cheese, resembling thick yogurt in texture but it is not as tangy as yogurt. Its fat content varies, some is virtually fat free, others contain up to eight per cent fat. Plain fromage frais is very versatile and can be used in cooking or served instead of cream with desserts. Fromage frais does not whip but it is thick and can be folded in.

Herbs

Buy freeze-dried herbs if you cannot find fresh but remember the flavour of most herbs is about twice as strong when they are dried as when they are fresh. If possible, look for dried whole leaf herbs in preference to chopped herbs and store in a sealed container in a cool, dry place away from light. Ordinary dried herbs should be used within six to nine months as they lose their flavour.

Mushrooms

On no account should you pick wild mushrooms unless you can positively identify them or you are with an expert. Some fungi are deadly poisonous and others will make you ill. It is easy to confuse edible varieties with non-edible.
Field mushrooms are the most commonly found wild mushrooms in Britain, others include the blewits, chanterelle, honey fungus, the horse mushroom, morel, orange peel fungus, oyster

mushroom and parasol mushroom. Some larger supermarkets are now stocking cultivated 'wild' mushrooms so take a look next time you are there. Their taste is certainly worth the search.

Oyster: these are shaped like a fan and have a smooth, slippery texture reminiscent of an oyster. They have a slightly meatier flavour than the mushrooms we are used to. Tear the caps into long triangular pieces following the lines of the gills.

Nutmeg

Whole nutmeg is hard and brown with a woody texture. It has a warm, sweet, nutty flavour. Grate at the last minute because the flavour is quickly lost. If you use nutmeg a lot it's worth investing in a nutmeg grater – some even provide storage space to keep the nutmegs fresh.

Okra

Known as 'ladies' fingers', these five-sided edible seed pods are normally between 7.5-10cm/3-4in long. Choose small, firm, bright green ones that do not bend. Avoid any with brown spots. Always wash okra before trimming and cutting. Okra contains a sticky juice that is released when the pod is cut. When sliced and cooked, this gelatinous quality helps to thicken dishes such as gumbo and gives a silky finish to soups and stews.

Peppers

Originally you could only buy green, then red peppers, which are a riper version of the green but new strains with vivid colours are appearing on supermarket shelves. Take your pick from yellow, white, orange and even black. Look for shiny, bright and firm unwrinkled skins and avoid any with any soft spots. They keep well in the fridge packed in a plastic bag.

Potatoes

Cara: a large, round main-crop with creamy flesh, this is a good all-rounder.

Desirée: a very popular, red-skinned main-crop with pale yellow flesh, this is an excellent all-rounder. It is particularly good for mashing and roasting and firm enough for salads.

King Edward: a large main-crop with a pale skin and pink flashes, this has cream-coloured, floury-textured flesh and is an excellent all-rounder.

Pentland Squire: a main-crop with white skin and white flesh, this has a floury texture. It is perfect for baking, boiling and mashing.

Romano: a popular main-crop with red skin and cream flesh, it is suitable for all cooking methods.

Spanish onions

These onions have the largest bulbs and are much milder than ordinary brown onions. They do not necessarily come from Spain and may be brown or red-skinned. Choose firm, dry onions with thin, light skins. Avoid any that are soft, show signs of dampness or are sprouting.

Turmeric

A fresh turmeric root looks exactly like ginger but it is bright orange inside the peel. You will find it more often sold ground. It has an aromatic, slightly bitter flavour and should be used sparingly. Be careful when handling, as it can stain your hands.

1. Trout
2. Salmon fillet
3. Smoked haddock
4. Cod fillet
5. Oysters
6. Mussels
7. Peppers
8. Emmenthal
9. Gruyère
10. Potatoes
11. Okra
12. Fromage frais
13. Fresh bay leaves
14. Dried bay leaves
15. Anchovies
16. Chanterelle mushrooms
17. Yellow oyster mushrooms
18. Grey oyster mushrooms
19. Spanish onion
20. Haricot beans
21. Dried parsley
22. Suet
23. Treacle
24. Fennel
25. Couscous
26. Turmeric
27. Chestnuts
28. Saffron
29. Raw prawns
30. Chick peas
31. Dried chives
32. Goat's cheese

Soups & Starters

CULLEN SKINK

Despite its extraordinary name, this is a Scottish soup of great distinction and long pedigree. It can be served either in chunks, for a hearty meal-type soup or blended in a food processor for a substantial, but more delicate first course.

Serves 4

225g/8oz smoked haddock, with or without bones (See Crafty Tip)

600ml/1 pint milk

450g/1lb waxy firm potatoes, such as Desirée or Pentland Squire, cut into 1cm/½in cubes

225g/8oz onions, cut into 1cm/½in cubes

2 tbsp chopped fresh parsley, to garnish

1 Cut the fish into moderate-sized pieces, place in a large pan with the milk and 450ml/16fl oz of water. Bring to the boil and simmer very gently for 15 minutes or until the fish comes off the bone and flakes easily.

2 Using a slotted spoon, remove fish and leave liquid in the pan. Add the potatoes and onions to the pan, bring to the boil and simmer, covered, for 10 minutes.

3 Separate the fish pieces from bones and skin, then add the flesh to the pan to heat through. Liquidise at this point, if you wish. Serve garnished with parsley.

Nutrition notes per serving: *250 calories, Protein 18g, Carbohydrate 31g, Fat 7g, Saturated fat 4g, Fibre 3g, Added sugar none, Salt 1.91g.*

CRAFTY TIP

You will need to decide between smoked haddock that has no colouring in it (apart from that naturally produced by the smoke) and the bright golden kind. My vote is clearly for the one in which the colour is natural.

CRAFTY PEPERONI WITH GOATS' CHEESE Ⓥ

Use at least two colours of pepper for this Italian-style salad. They should be completely cold before serving. Store in the fridge for up to 12 hours before adding the goats' cheese.

Serves 4

750g/1lb 10oz mixed peppers, halved and seeded

2 tbsp olive oil

1 garlic clove, finely chopped

salt and freshly ground black pepper

juice of 1 lemon

1 x 55–85g/2–3oz 'round' goats' cheese

25g/1oz chopped fresh parsley

1 Slice the peppers across into 5mm/¼in strips. Heat the oil in a frying pan wide enough to take all the peppers. Add the garlic and pepper slices and toss over a medium to high heat for 2–3 minutes. Season, reduce the heat and gently cook the peppers for 10 minutes or until they are just beginning to caramelise. Squeeze over the lemon juice, turn to coat and leave to cool.

2 Cut the goats' cheese into four slices across the round and dip one side into the parsley. Transfer the peppers to a serving dish and arrange the goats' cheese, parsley side up, on top.

Nutrition notes per serving: *124 calories, Protein 4g, Carbohydrate 10g, Fat 8g,*

FRENCH VEGETABLE SOUP Ⓥ ✳

A simple but perfect formula. Fresh ingredients mixed in the right proportions, cooked in the classic way and served without delay.

Serves 4

25g/1oz butter

225g/8oz leeks, chopped

225g/8oz potatoes, chopped

225g/8oz carrots, chopped

salt and freshly ground black pepper

1 litre/1¾ pints water or vegetable stock

chopped fresh parsley, to garnish

1 Melt the butter in a pan, then add the leeks, potatoes and carrots. Stir for 2-3 minutes to coat the vegetables, season, then add the water or stock and simmer for 20 minutes.

2 Transfer to a food processor or blender and process until blended but still with some texture. (It can also be served without liquidising, if you prefer.) Spoon into bowls and sprinkle with parsley.

Nutrition notes per serving: *128 calories, Protein 4g, Carbohydrate 16g, Fat 6g, Saturated fat 3g, Fibre 3g, Added sugar none, Salt 1.24g.*

✳ *Cool quickly, then freeze. Can be frozen for up to 1 month. To serve, defrost in the fridge, reheat until piping hot, then garnish with parsley.*

CAESAR SALAD

This can be eaten with meat or fish dishes but is wonderful served as a starter on its own.

Serves 6

1 large cos or iceberg lettuce, leaves separated

55g can anchovy fillets, drained and sliced

3 tbsp olive oil

1 garlic clove, crushed

115g/4oz white bread, cut into cubes

25g/1oz Parmesan, freshly grated

FOR THE DRESSING

3 tbsp salad oil

1 tbsp fresh lemon juice

1 egg, boiled for 1 minute and scooped out or 2 tbsp fromage frais (See Crafty Tip)

¼ tsp sugar

salt and freshly ground black pepper

1 Break the lettuce into bite-sized pieces and add the anchovy fillets. Heat the oil in a frying pan and add the garlic and bread cubes. Fry the croûtons over a medium heat for 2 minutes until golden and crisp, then drain on kitchen paper. Discard the garlic.

2 Make the dressing: place all the ingredients in a bowl and whisk well until thick and creamy. Pour over the lettuce and anchovies, add the croûtons, then sprinkle with the Parmesan. Toss well before serving.

Nutrition notes per serving: *214 calories, Protein 7g, Carbohydrate 11g, Fat 16g, Saturated fat 3g, Fibre 1g, Added sugar 1g, Salt 1.28g.*

Ⓥ Vegetarian option: *leave out the anchovies and add extra Parmesan cheese.*

CRAFTY TIP

The classic Caesar salad dressing is made with a 1-minute boiled egg (rather like an unthickened mayonnaise) but with salmonella scares in mind, you may wish to play safe and substitute a little yogurt or fromage frais.

PIPERADE Ⓥ

This dish began life in the Basque country as a peasant recipe using local ingredients. It's not an omelette. It's meant to be a kind of grand vegetable scrambled egg and is best served in small bowls with hot French bread. It is also good eaten cold as an hors d'oeuvre.

Serves 4

2 tbsp olive oil

2 large red peppers and 1 large green pepper, seeded and thinly sliced

225g/8oz Spanish onions, thinly sliced

225g/8oz large tomatoes

1 garlic clove, finely chopped

25g/1oz butter

salt and freshly ground black pepper

6 eggs, beaten

juice of ½ lemon

1 Heat the olive oil in a non-stick or well-seasoned heavy-based pan and gently fry the peppers and onions for 5–7 minutes until softened but not browned. Halve the tomatoes, scoop out and discard any seeds, then thinly slice. Add to the pan with the garlic and butter.

2 Season the vegetables generously and add the eggs to the pan, scrambling them continuously over a medium heat until they are creamy but not set hard. Add the lemon juice, stir one last time and serve before the eggs overcook and become totally firm.

Nutrition notes per serving: *271 calories, Protein 12g, Carbohydrate 13g, Fat 19g, Saturated fat 6g, Fibre 3g, Added sugar none, Salt 0.66g.*

VICHYSSOISE

This soup is delicious and surprisingly enough very pleasant eaten in cold weather before a hearty meal, as well as in high summer.

Serves 4

450g/1lb leeks (See Crafty Tip)

2 tbsp oil

450g/1lb potatoes, cut into cubes

salt and freshly ground black pepper

1.2 litres/2 pints chicken stock

6 tbsp double cream

chopped fresh parsley, to garnish

1 Trim the leeks, keeping as much of the green part as you can. Split and wash in lots of cold water to get rid of any sand or grit, then cut into 2.5cm/1in pieces.

2 Heat the oil in a pan and gently fry the potatoes and leeks for 5 minutes, without browning. Season generously, add the stock, bring to the boil and simmer until the vegetables are soft.

3 Liquidise or process in a food processor until smooth. Add the cream, stir and pour into a bowl to cool. The soup can be placed in the fridge once it's below blood heat (that means you can put your finger in without screaming). Stir thoroughly before serving, garnished with parsley.

Nutrition notes per serving: *269 calories, Protein 6g, Carbohydrate 24g, Fat 17g, Saturated fat 7g, Fibre 4g, Added sugar none, Salt 1.28g.*

CRAFTY TIP

Watercress is often substituted for leeks in modern versions of this soup. It provides a brighter colour but not such a subtle taste. You can use fromage frais instead of the double cream, although it gives the soup a slightly sharper flavour.

Meat

STEAK IN CREAM SAUCE

Don't let on how easy this sauce is to make. No one can ever believe it when they taste it, and I've been getting away with it for years. This is one of the earliest of the crafty cooking recipes from *Food & Drink* and it's still one of the all-time favourites. This technique, using cream as a sauce with sautéed meat, is especially good with steaks but it also works a treat with other meats and other flavours. Sauté chicken breasts and flavour the cream with snipped chives instead of mustard, or try veal escalopes (make sure the calves were raised in the humane British way) and add juniper berries to the cream.

For each person

salt and freshly ground black pepper

1 entrecôte or sirloin steak (See Crafty Tip)

generous knob of butter

a little oil

2 tbsp double cream

1 tsp grain mustard

1 Season the steak. Heat the butter and oil in a heavy frying pan until foaming. Add the steak and fry over a high heat on one side for 2 minutes. Turn over, add the cream and stir in the mustard. Cook for 1 minute more, then serve.

Nutrition notes per serving: *603 calories, Protein 52g, Carbohydrate 1g, Fat 43g, Saturated fat 22g, Fibre 1g, Added sugar none, Salt 1.57g.*

CRAFTY TIP

Cuts of beef vary from country to country because of the way the carcase is butchered. The same is also true within Britain where there are also regional variations. Whichever steak you choose to cook make sure it is well-hung. It should be almost maroon in colour and been aged for two to three weeks before you buy it. Fresh or mature, the flesh will be slightly moist with white or creamy-white fat. Freshly slaughtered meat is bright coral red and when cooked tends to have very little taste. During hanging it matures and its flavour and texture develops. Sirloin steaks are tender, juicy prime steaks from the back or loin which is the most tender part of the animal. They contain a marbling of fat (which helps keep the meat moist and tender during cooking) as well as an outer layer of fat. Entrecôte, a classic French steak, cut from 'between the ribs' in the middle part of a sirloin of beef, are thick, juicy and well-marbled. Steaks need very little preparation before cooking. Wipe well and trim off excess fat but do not remove it all. Slash the remaining fat at intervals before cooking to prevent the edges of the meat curling while it is frying.

HUNGARIAN GOULASH ✸

My friend and colleague Egon Ronay, one of the great leading lights of British gastronomy for more than 20 years, devotes two pages of one of his books to 'the original authentic gulyas' saying that never has a culinary term been so abused and degraded. I hope he won't feel that the crafty version below degrades this romantic Hungarian dish. His key point, I think, is that it should be made with the best quality paprika. Known in the business as 'sweet noble', it is not hot and spicy, but full and rich. It's worth finding a specialist grocer who sells it. Otherwise this goulash is not too difficult a dish to achieve. This is certainly one of the easiest and most heartening casseroles I know. A complete meal in itself, it calls for soup bowls, chunks of wholemeal bread and hearty appetites. Or you could serve it with noodles and a little soured cream. If you dont' have any soured cream, add one tablespoon of fresh lemon juice to 150ml/¼pint single cream and stir well. The texture and taste are not exactly the same but it is a reasonable substitute.

Serves 6

1 tbsp oil

900g lean beef, cut into cubes

2 onions, sliced

4 tbsp tomato purée

1 tbsp paprika (See Crafty Tip)

750g/1lb 10oz potatoes, cut into walnut-sized chunks

1 tsp caraway seeds

salt and freshly ground black pepper

1 tsp cornflour (optional)

1 Heat the oil in a heavy casserole or pan and brown the meat on all sides. Add the onions and cook over a medium heat until translucent, stirring from time to time. Add the tomato purée, paprika and enough water to cover. Simmer, covered, for 45 minutes.

2 Add the potatoes to the pan with the caraway seeds, season well and simmer, covered, for a further 20 minutes. If the sauce is too thin, add the cornflour mixed with a little water and stir until the sauce thickens, or remove one or two of the potatoes, mash, then return them to the sauce.

Nutrition notes per serving: *329 calories, Protein 35g, Carbohydrate 28g, Fat 10g, Saturated fat 3g, Fibre 2g, Added sugar none, Salt 0.49g.*

✸ *Cool quickly, then freeze. Can be frozen for up to 1 month. To serve, defrost in the fridge and reheat until piping hot.*

CRAFTY TIP

Paprika is the ground powder of dried ripe European sweet red peppers and adds the characteristicially rich red colour to many Austrian and Hungarian dishes including goulash. It is also used widely in Spain in sauces, sausages and in fish dishes. Mild and hot peppers are used to produce it, so check the label before buying. Quite often the seeds and cores are removed before the peppers are ground so it is much milder than its fiery chilli relations – cayenne and chilli powder. Buy little and often, it does not keep well.

SPRING LAMB STEW
(NAVARIN PRINTANIER) ✽

Lamb stews play only a small part in Britain's culinary tradition, but they are a world-wide phenomenon. This one from France was traditionally made in the spring. That was because spring lamb and the new vegetables arrived at the same time. By my reckoning, that must have been in June, a bit late for the average spring. No matter. The combination of lamb and vegetables is a delicious one. Some versions include new potatoes but I think they're best cooked separately, and eaten in their jackets, as otherwise there's nothing to contrast the flavours against.

Serves 6–8

1kg shoulder or boned breast of lamb, cut into 5x1cm/2x½in pieces

225g/8oz onions, cut into 1cm/½in slices

225g/8oz stringless green beans, topped, tailed and cut in half lengthways (See Crafty Tip)

225g/8oz carrots, cut into batons

225g/8oz turnips, cut into batons

2 celery sticks, cut into 1cm/½in slices

pinch of freeze-dried thyme

pinch of freeze-dried marjoram

salt and freshly ground black pepper

1 tbsp cornflour

1 tbsp tomato purée

1   Place the lamb, fat side down, in a sauté pan or flameproof casserole large enough to hold all the ingredients. Brown in its own fat over a gentle heat for 5 minutes. Add the onions and stir, then add enough water to come halfway up the meat pieces, cover and gently cook for 20 minutes, stirring occasionally.

2   Check the liquid is not drying out, then add the beans, carrots, turnips, celery and the herbs. Season generously and bring to a gentle boil, cover and simmer for 10 minutes.

3   Mix the cornflour with 250ml/9fl oz of water and the tomato purée until smooth. Using a slotted spoon, transfer the meat and vegetables to a serving dish.

4   Make the cooking juices up to about 300ml/½ pint with water, then add the tomato and cornflour mixture. Bring to the boil, stirring, until the sauce thickens, then pour over the meat. The dish should be quite liquid — it's really a stew.

Nutrition notes per serving: *460 calories, Protein 32g, Carbohydrate 13g, Fat 32g, Saturated fat 16g, Fibre 3g, Added sugar none, Salt 0.47g.*

✽ *Cool quickly, then freeze. Can be frozen for up to 1 month. To serve, defrost in the fridge and reheat until piping hot.*

CRAFTY TIP

When buying green beans choose small, slim beans with a rich green pod and a slight bloom. Check for freshness by snapping one in half – it should break cleanly and be juicy. If you do need to remove the string, nip off the top and pull the string down the pod, then repeat at the other end, pulling the string from the other side. Topping and tailing beans can seem like a lifetime's work – unless you do it the crafty way. Take a handful of beans, hold them vertically over a chopping board and shake them gently until the tip of each bean just touches the surface of the board. Now they are level, lay them flat and cut all the ends off at once. Turn the beans round and repeat the process.

BEEF AND KIDNEY PIE ✽

This is the pie version of one of the great British dishes – Steak and kidney pudding which is made in a basin with suet crust. A wonderful winter dish, this pie needs to be served with plenty of mashed potato and a green vegetable.

6 oysters (optional) (See Crafty Tip)

1 tbsp beef dripping or oil

750g stewing steak, cut into 2.5cm/1in cubes

225g lamb or ox kidney, cut into 1cm/½in cubes

1 large onion, chopped

1 heaped tbsp plain flour

225g/8oz button mushrooms, quartered

1 tbsp Worcestershire sauce

600ml/1 pint stock or water

salt and freshly ground black pepper

1 quantity Shortcrust pastry (page 62)

beaten egg, to glaze

1 Open the oysters, if using. Or ask your fishmonger to do it and bring the fish and their juices home in a tub. Place the dripping in a pan and brown the meat over a medium heat. Add the onion and toss for 1–2 minutes, then sprinkle on the flour, stirring, so that it takes up the juices.

2 If you are using oysters, add to the pan at this stage with the mushrooms and the Worcestershire sauce and enough stock or water to just cover the meat. Season generously and simmer for 30 minutes.

3 Preheat the oven to 300F/150C/Gas 2. Roll out the pastry to roughly the size needed to fit over a pie dish, cut out a 1cm/½in wide strip. Transfer the meat to the dish and check seasoning. Dampen the edge of the dish, place the pastry strip round the rim of the dish, then lay the rolled-out pastry on top to cover the dish, crimping down to secure. Slash a couple of holes in the middle to let out the steam, decorate with pastry trimmings, if you like, and brush with beaten egg.

4 Bake for 1½ hours. You may want to put a piece of greaseproof paper over the top of the pie after the first 30 minutes to stop it browning too quickly before the meat is cooked.

Nutrition notes per serving: *803 calories, Protein 60g, Carbohydrate 56g, Fat 39g, Saturated fat 21g, Fibre 3g, Added sugar 4g, Salt 3.47g.*

✽ *Cool the meat quickly, then freeze. Can be frozen for up to 1 month. To serve, defrost in the fridge, then cover with pastry, glaze and bake. You can also freeze the cooked pie. Simply defrost, then reheat, covered with foil, until piping hot. If you prefer cover meat with the pastry, freeze and cook after defrosting.*

CRAFTY TIP

Oysters are available these days even when there isn't a letter 'r' in the month, but they are simply not as good as when there is. When buying live oysters, check the shells are firmly closed. Scrub well. To split them (known as shucking) use a special oyster knife with a broad wooden handle that fits into the palm of the hand and which has a short heavy-duty blade. Grip the oyster firmly in a cloth in the palm of your hand, insert the knife into the hinged edge and twist to prise open the shells. Still holding the shell firmly, slide the knife along the inside of the upper shell to sever the first of two muscles. Lift off the upper shell, then slide the knife under the oyster in the lower shell to sever the second muscle.

MEDITERRANEAN KEBABS

The method of cooking kebabs is very similar throughout the eastern Mediterranean and it's also very, very simple. This is a version for eating in summer and preferably outdoors, or at least at a time to recapture the memory of warmer days. Serve the kebabs with a salad made from tomatoes, feta cheese and herbs and with hot pittas or crusty flat bread coated in toasted sesame seeds, and even a wet December night in the Midlands can have a whiff of sun-baked hills. If you are using wooden bamboo skewers, soak them first in a bowl of water so that they do not catch light under the grill. Metal skewers with flat sides are the best ones to use as they make it easy to turn the meat as it cooks.

Serves 4

1 Spanish onion

750g boned leg or shoulder of lamb, cut into walnut-sized pieces

4 tbsp olive oil

juice of 1 lemon

1 tsp freeze-dried oregano

1 tsp freeze-dried thyme

8 bay leaves

1 red pepper and 1 green pepper, seeded and cut into 4cm/1½in squares

1 Quarter the onion, then vertically halve the pieces and halve again to get 16 chunks. Roughly chop any stray pieces including the core. Place the chopped onion on the lamb pieces, pour over the olive oil and lemon juice and mix in the herbs. Cover and leave to marinate in the fridge for at least 2 hours. Up to 12 hours will do no harm.

2 Preheat the grill to maximum, line the grill pan with foil and thread the lamb, onion chunks, bay leaves and pepper squares on to skewers. Pack reasonably tight together at the sharp end of the skewer. Grill for 6–7 minutes each side, basting with the marinade. When cooked the meat should be crisp and brown on the outside but soft and succulent inside and the vegetables should be singed but not burned.

Nutrition notes per serving: *512 calories, Protein 38g, Carbohydrate 7g, Fat 37g, Saturated fat 14g, Fibre 2g, Added sugar none, Salt 0.35g.*

CRAFTY TIP

If you would like to spice up the lamb Indian-style, mix together the chopped onion with one dessertspoon of mild curry powder and one garlic clove crushed with a teaspoon of salt. Add the lemon juice, beat in 150ml/¼pint of natural yogurt and use as a marinade for the lamb. Remove the lamb from the marinade and scrape off any bits and pieces before threading on to skewers and grilling. Discard the marinade.

Poultry

CHICKEN WITH A SATAY PEANUT SAUCE

This sauce is a crafty adaptation of a sauce that's enormously popular all over South-east Asia – Malaysia, Indonesia, Thailand all have their own versions. This is made with peanut butter rather than starting with whole peanuts. It's delicious with chicken, but I have to say it goes well with almost all grilled meats. The chicken can be cooked under the grill or on a barbecue. If you put the lime in the microwave for 10 seconds on HIGH it will give lots more juice. This also applies to lemons.

Serves 4

12 chicken drumsticks

4 tbsp (light) soy sauce

55g/2oz (light) muscovado sugar (See Crafty Tip)

juice of 1½ limes (See Crafty Tip)

1 tbsp cooking oil (not olive)

1 garlic clove, crushed with 1 tsp salt

115g/4oz crunchy peanut butter

1 generous tsp chilli sauce

rice salad or jacket potatoes, to serve

1 Place the drumsticks in a non-metallic bowl. Mix togther the soy sauce, sugar, lime juice, oil and garlic and pour over the chicken and leave to marinate, covered in the fridge, for as little as 30 minutes or as a long as 12 hours.

2 Preheat the grill or barbecue. Using a slotted spoon, remove the chicken from the marinade and grill or barbecue for 5–6 minutes each side until cooked through. Test with a skewer or sharp knife, the juices should run clear.

3 Meanwhile, place the marinade in a non-stick pan with the peanut butter and 150ml/¼ pint of water. Bring to the boil and stir. It will look extremely unpromising at first but as it starts to boil it will blend together into a smooth golden sauce. Add the chilli sauce to taste and simmer until the drumsticks are ready. Serve the drumsticks with a little sauce poured over and extra on the side with a rice salad or jacket potatoes.

Nutrition notes per serving: *588 calories, Protein 33g, Carbohydrate 18g, Fat 43g, Saturated fat 8g, Fibre 2g, Added sugar 14g, Salt 0.52g.*

CRAFTY TIP

Soy sauce with its salty, sweetish taste, is an essential ingredient in Chinese and other types of Asian cooking. It is made from soya beans which have been boiled, flour and water and then naturally fermented. Good quality soy is aged from six months to two years so that the sauce matures and the flavour develops. Light soy sauce is full of flavour and the best one to use for cooking. Dark soy sauce is cooked, resulting in its darker, almost black colour. Dark soy is slightly thicker and stronger than light soy sauce and more suited to dishes requiring more robust seasoning. Use both with caution to avoid oversalting. Stored tightly sealed and away from light, soy sauce will keep for six months at room temperature. It will darken and become more concentrated over time.

NORMANDY CHICKEN

In Normandy, in northern France, there is a valley called the Auge, famous for its apples and its cream. This recipe is a product of both. I've adapted it to include fresh apple juice creating a wonderful mixture of richness, sharpness and sweetness.

1 tbsp oil

4 chicken joints (See Crafty Tip)

½ Spanish onion, chopped

salt and freshly ground black pepper

300ml/½ pint fresh apple juice

25g/1oz butter

2 Cox's apples, cored but not peeled

1 tsp cornflour

150ml/¼ pint double cream

chopped fresh parsley, to garnish

1   Preheat the oven to 350F/180C/Gas 4. Heat the oil in a frying pan and add the chicken joints and onion. Cook for 10 minutes over a medium heat until the chicken pieces are browned on both sides and the onions are translucent. Transfer to a casserole and season. Pour enough apple juice to come almost halfway up the chicken and cook in the oven for 25 minutes. The chicken can also be simmered on top of the oven in the frying pan, covered, for the same length of time.

2   Meanwhile, gently melt the butter in another frying pan. Cut each apple into 12 segments and fry over a high heat for 3–4 minutes or until golden. Keep warm.

3   Using a slotted spoon, remove the chicken pieces and keep warm. Add the cornflour to the cream and stir together. Blend into the chicken pan juices and heat gently until the liquid has thickened. Place the fried apples and the chicken pieces on a serving dish, pour over the sauce and garnish with parsley.

Nutrition notes per serving: *553 calories, Protein 20g, Carbohydrate 18g, Fat 45g, Saturated fat 21g, Fibre 2g, Added sugar none, Salt 0.60g.*

CRAFTY TIP

It is usually cheaper to buy a whole chicken and cut it up yourself into portions and use the bones and trimmings for stock. Remove all the trussing strings. With the bird breast side up, cut through the skin between the leg and breast. Bend the leg back until it cracks and remove the leg by cutting through the joint. Repeat on the other side. Separate the thighs from the drumsticks by bending the leg to crack the joint and cut through with a sharp knife. (You will find a line of fat over the joint. If you follow this line carefully, you'll be amazed at how easy it is to cut through.) Remove the wings by bending back and drawing around the base of each wing with the knife, cutting to the bone. Twist and separate the joint with the knife. Carefully cut down one side of the breast bone and scrape away the meat from the carcase to remove one breast, then repeat on the other side.

CHICKEN FLORENTINE

This classic combination of spinach and cheese comes from Florence and traditionally accompanies fish or eggs, but I find it particularly good with chicken.

TV Cooks MICHAEL BARRY COOKS CRAFTY CLASSICS

Serves 4

2 chicken breasts and 2 thighs

1 bay leaf

1 onion, left whole

450g/1lb fresh spinach, blanched (See Crafty Tip)

knob of butter, melted

FOR THE SAUCE

300ml/½ pint milk

25g/1oz butter

25g/1oz plain flour

½ tsp freshly grated nutmeg

115g/4oz Gruyère or Cheddar cheese, grated

1 Poach the chicken pieces for 20 minutes in 300ml/½ pint of water with the bay leaf and onion, then leave to cool.

2 Preheat the oven to 375F/190C/Gas 5. Meanwhile, make the sauce: whisk the milk, butter and flour together in a pan over a medium heat until thick.

3 Bone and skin the chicken pieces, leaving the flesh in large pieces. Toss the spinach in the melted butter and line an ovenproof dish with the mixture. Lay the chicken on top in a single layer. Mix the nutmeg and 85g/3oz of the cheese into the sauce. Pour over the chicken, sprinkle with the remaining cheese and bake for 15 minutes until the cheese sauce bubbles.

Nutrition notes per serving: *538 calories, Protein 33g, Carbohydrate 13g, Fat 40g, Saturated fat 18g, Fibre 3g, Added sugar none, Salt 1.35g.*

CRAFTY TIP

You can use frozen leaf spinach if you must, but there is no comparison with fresh leaves blanched in boiling water for 30 seconds before use. Fresh spinach is available all year, with home-grown in season early and late summer. Delicately flavoured summer spinach is light green with tender leaves and stalks. Winter spinach is much darker, has coarser-textured leaves and stalks and a much stronger flavour. Avoid any with yellowing or damaged leaves. If possible choose small to medium leaves with thin stalks. Always use spinach within a day or two of buying – it will keep in the fridge overnight in a polythene bag. To prepare, wash in several changes of water to remove any soil and grit and shake dry. Handle leaves with care as they bruise easily. Remove any tough central ribs. With one hand, fold the leaf in half with the stalk upwards and the ridge outwards. With the other, tear the stalk from the leaf. After cooking, drain well and press the water out of the leaves with the back of a wooden spoon.

PAELLA

Paella, the most famous of all Spanish dishes, is a fabulous celebratory meal. Like its cousin the pilau, paella is a rice-based dish, but one that is adventurous in its mixing of flavours, meat and fish, spices and herbs. In Spain, it is eaten as a family dish and it certainly seems best shared round a table, with time to enjoy it. It can be cooked in any big open pan. Saffron, the most expensive spice in the world, has a strong, slightly bitter flavour and a pungent sweet scent. If you are using saffron strands, infuse a few in a little boiling water to extract the flavour and brilliant yellow colour, then stir into the rice. Do not use too much, it can be overpowering if you are not used to it.

Serves 6

9 chicken joints, weighing about 1.5–2kg

4 tbsp olive oil

225g/8oz onions, finely chopped

1 garlic clove, finely chopped

280g/10oz long grain rice

1 tsp chopped fresh thyme or ½ tsp freeze-dried

1 tsp chopped fresh rosemary or ½ tsp freeze-dried

1 packet saffron powder

225g/8oz French beans, cut into large dice

1 red pepper, seeded and cut into large dice

600ml/1 pint mussels, washed and scraped (See Crafty tip, page 37)

225g/8oz cooked prawns, peeled or with their shells (See Crafty Tip)

225g/8oz frozen peas

1 Fry the chicken joints gently in the oil until golden, then add the onions and garlic. Measure the rice by volume, add to the pan, then add twice the measure of water. Stir in the thyme, rosemary and saffron. Simmer for 25 minutes. You can cover the pan with a lid or piece of foil, though it's not traditional.

2 Place the beans, pepper, mussels, prawns and peas on top of the rice and cook for 10 minutes, uncovered. Discard any mussels that do not open. Stir gently and serve the paella in the dish in which it was cooked.

Nutrition notes per serving: *721 calories, Protein 47g, Carbohydrate 50g, Fat 38g, Saturated fat 10g, Fibre 4g, Added sugar none, Salt 2.04g.*

CRAFTY TIP

Prawns vary in size from 5–18cm/2–7in in length. They are usually cooked immediately they are caught with or without their shells.and frozen with a thin coating of ice. Defrost in the fridge in a covered dish, drain well (they usually contain a lot of water), then pat dry with kitchen paper before using. To peel prawns: hold the head and tail end, using your thumb and forefinger and pull off the head. Remove the body shell and claws from underneath, slipping off sideways, then pull off the tail. Using the point of a knife, carefully remove the black vein running down the back. Reheat cooked prawns thoroughly but be careful not to overcook, as they will toughen.

CHICKEN TIKKA ✻

This is India's classic grilled-chicken dish. Eat with flat Indian bread (such as naan) and yogurt chutney and serve with sliced lettuce, lemon quarters and caramelised onions. To caramelise onions: thinly slice, then fry in very hot shallow oil until crispy. Keep stirring them or they will burn. To make Crafty yogurt chutney: mix together 140g/5oz of natural yogurt, a 5cm/2in piece of grated cucumber and two teaspoons of concentrated mint sauce. Leave for 30 minutes before serving.

Serves 4–6

6 boneless skinless chicken breasts, cut into smallish pieces

FOR THE MARINADE

140g/5oz natural yogurt

½ Spanish onion, sliced

juice of ½ lemon

2–3 garlic cloves, chopped

2 tsp turmeric

2 tsp ground cumin (See Crafty Tip)

1 tsp ground ginger or 1 heaped tsp chopped fresh root ginger

1 tsp chilli powder

2 good tsp ground coriander (See Crafty Tip)

2 bay leaves

1 Mix the marinade ingredients together in a large bowl and add the chicken pieces. Cover and chill for 6 hours or longer.

2 Preheat the oven to 450F/230C/Gas 8. Remove the chicken from the marinade, discarding any large pieces of onion that may have stuck to it and place on a raised wire rack over a baking tray. Sprinkle with a little salt and bake   for 30–40 minutes until brown and crisp on the outside and soft in the middle.

Nutrition notes per serving for four: *317 calories, Protein 53g, Carbohydrate 8g, Fat 8g, Saturated fat 3g, Fibre 1g, Added sugar none, Salt 0.78g.*

✻ *Cool the cooked tikka, then freeze. Can be frozen for up to 1 month. To serve, defrost in the fridge, then reheat, covered with foil, until piping hot or eat cold.*

CRAFTY TIP

The spice trail: cumin are the small, ridged seeds of a plant related to parsley. They have a strong, earthy aromatic fragrance and can be bought whole or ground. Cumin is also an ingredient of curry powders and some chilli powder mixtures. Coriander is an important ingredient in Indian and South-East Asian cooking. The small, round, brown seeds of the coriander plant are sold whole or powdered. They have a mild, sweet orangey flavour and are an ingredient found in most curry powders.

Fish & Shellfish

MOULES MARINIÈRE

This most famous of all mussel dishes comes from France and literally means 'sailor's mussels'. A purist might actually call my recipes Moules à la crème, but I've eaten Moules marinière with and without cream all round the French coast. The apple juice provides just a touch of sweetness in the sauce to match the natural sweetness of good fresh mussels.

Serves 2–3

1 garlic clove, chopped

175ml/6fl oz fresh apple juice

1.2 litres/2 pints fresh mussels, cleaned (See Crafty Tip)

salt and freshly ground black pepper

1 tsp cornflour

150ml/¼ pint double or single cream

chopped fresh parsley, to garnish

1 Place the garlic, apple juice and mussels in a pan and season. Bring to the boil, cover and simmer for 5 minutes, shaking the pan frequently. The mussels will open when cooked – discard any that do not.

2 Mix the cornflour into the cream, add to the pan and stir. Bring back to the boil, shake again and cook for 1 minute. Spoon the mussels and sauce into bowls and sprinkle with parsley.

Nutrition notes per serving for two: *502 calories, Protein 24g, Carbohydrate 14g, Fat 40g, Saturated fat 23g, Fibre 1g, Added sugar none, Salt 1.90g.*

CRAFTY TIP

Fresh mussels are at their most delicious in March. Make sure they are alive when you buy them – they should be tightly shut. Discard any that are open and do not close when tapped sharply, and any with broken or cracked shells or loose hinges. To clean: thoroughly scrub the outside before cooking and remove the beard. Leave for 1–2 hours in a bucket of clean, salted water to clean internally. Discard any mussels that float to the top. Our shores grow some of the finest shellfish in the world, though pollution and carelessness have threatened many of our best sources. Mussels are still one of our cheapest delicacies, although the ones in the shops tend to come from Ireland or even Spain these days. The enterprising packers from these countries calculated that if they cleaned the shells most of the work (and disincentive for the cook) would be done and cleaned mussels can now be bought in packs from larger supermarkets.

TROUT WITH ALMONDS
(TRUITE AUX AMANDES)

With fresh farm trout so widely available, I think they make a particularly attractive introduction to fish for people who are worried about bones. Trout have only a few, which are very tidily arranged. If anyone is put off by the bones, it's a fair bet they will also be worried about the heads, so don't be affected by the old-fashioned belief that you're meant to serve trout with the heads on. If you, or your family or friends, think a reproachful stare from the plate is not conductive to a good appetite, cut the heads off before you coat the fish in the almonds. The combination of trout and almonds is a classic and this version doubles the almonds. This is good with steamed cucumber pieces tossed in a little butter. Let your fishmonger clean and gut the trout for you.

Serves 4

115g/4oz ground almonds

4 trout, (See Crafty Tip)

2 tbsp oil

55g/2oz butter

25g/1oz slivered almonds

2 tbsp fresh lemon juice

1 Place the ground almonds in a plastic bag and shake each trout in the bag to coat thoroughly. Heat the oil in a large frying pan and gently fry the trout for 5 minutes on each side, then remove and keep warm.

2 Add the butter to the pan, turn up the heat and cook the slivered almonds until just brown. Add the lemon juice, then spoon over the trout and serve.

Nutrition notes per serving: *570 calories, Protein 43g, Carbohydrate 3g, Fat 43g, Saturated fat 11g, Fibre 3g, Added sugar none, Salt 0.61g.*

CRAFTY TIP

There are several different varieties of this popular freshwater fish – sea or salmon trout, rainbow and river or brown trout. The rainbow trout, spends all its life in freshwater, is readily available all year and is reared on trout farms. The delicate-flavoured flesh can be white or pink. Some fed on shrimps have a pinkish-red flesh and can be called 'red trout'. Rainbow trout is sold and usually cooked whole. Sea or salmon trout is bigger and has spent a season or more at sea, living on a diet or crustaceans and its flesh takes on a pink colour and flavour similar to salmon. River or brown trout is a delicacy not to be missed. A golden brown fish with whitish flesh it spends all its life in rivers and streams and is considered to have a better flavour than rainbow trout. It is at its best from March to September, although it is, unfortunately, rarely found in the shops. Snap it up if you find any.

COD IN PARSLEY SAUCE

Many of us have bitter memories of fish cooked in parsley sauce from our schooldays, but properly made it can be a great treat – the fresh tang of the parsley balancing the richness of the white sauce and complementing the flaky meatiness of fresh cod. In fact, properly done, you realise why it was one of the most popular dishes in Victorian times and why it was emulated so widely and catastrophically in so many school dining halls. Serve with new or mashed potatoes and simple vegetable such as carrots or stringless beans.

Serves 4

675g/1½lb skinless cod fillet

1 tbsp salt

FOR THE SAUCE

300ml/½ pint milk

150ml/¼ pint single cream

40g/1½oz plain flour

40g/1½oz butter, cut into cubes

salt and freshly ground black pepper

generous pinch of freshly grated nutmeg

85g/3oz finely chopped fresh parsley

juice of ½ lemon

1 Place the fish in a colander, set over a basin, and sprinkle with the salt. Leave for 20 minutes, then rinse thoroughly. This firms up the flesh. Place 5cm/2in of water in a large pan into which the colander will fit without touching the water. Bring the water to the boil, place the fish, still in the colander, in the pan and cover. Steam for 15 minutes or until the cod is just done but still succulent. (See Crafty Tip.)

2 Meanwhile, make the sauce: whisk together the milk, cream, flour and butter and bring gently to the boil. Make sure you're whisking at the moment the liquid comes to the boil and you will have a perfectly smooth and glossy sauce. Check seasoning, add the nutmeg, parsley and lemon juice. Carefully remove the cod to a serving dish and coat with the sauce.

Nutrition notes per serving: *364 calories, Protein 33g, Carbohydrate 14g, Fat 20g, Saturated fat 12g, Fibre 1g, Added sugar none, Salt 1.42g.*

CRAFTY TIP

When the fish is cooked it should be firm to the touch and just flaking. The thicker the fillet is the longer it will take to cook. Keep an eye on it, do not overcook or it will become tough and tasteless.

SALMON EN CROÛTE

This is perhaps the most popular fish dish we've ever done on *Food & Drink*. It comes out looking spectacular for remarkably little work. I always use ready-made puff pastry. You don't have to serve two sauces, of course, that's just being flashy. Serve with seasonal vegetables.

Serves 6–8

350g/12oz white fish (haddock, whiting or cod)

175g/6oz fresh white breadcrumbs

juice and grated rind of 1 lemon

1 tbsp snipped fresh chives

1 tbsp chopped fresh parsley

1 egg

4 tbsp sunflower oil

salt and freshly ground black pepper

450g/1lb puff pastry, thawed if frozen

2 x 400–450g/14oz–1lb skinless salmon fillets (See Crafty Tip)

beaten egg, to glaze

FOR THE CUCUMBER SAUCE

½ large cucumber, grated

115g/4oz fromage frais

FOR THE LEMON CREAM SAUCE

fish trimmings (See Crafty Tip)

juice of ½ lemon

1 bay leaf

4 peppercorns

4 tbsp double cream

1 Preheat the oven to 400F/200C/Gas 6. Place the white fish, breadcrumbs, lemon juice and rind, herbs, egg and oil into a food processor and whizz until smooth. Season well.

2 Roll out the pastry on a lightly floured surface into a long oval shape 15cm/6in longer than the salmon fillets and about one and a half times wider. Place one fillet in the middle of the pastry, spread with the white fish paste and sandwich with the other salmon fillet. Cut diagonal lines along each side of the puff pastry about 1cm/½in apart, leaving 7.5cm/3in at each end uncut.

3 Lift the pastry strips on either side of the salmon up and over the fish, criss-crossing over each other. Secure strips with beaten egg. Fold the flap of pastry at the top of the fish into a triangle to make the shape of a fish head, and cut a wedge from the bottom flap to make the shape of a tail.

4 Carefully lift the fish on to a greased baking sheet, brush with beaten egg and bake for 35–40 minutes. To check if the fish is cooked, insert a skewer between the plaits; it should come out clean. Serve plain or with one or both sauces.

5 Make the cucumber sauce: sprinkle the cucumber with salt and leave for 15 minutes for the excess water to drain out. Rinse and pat dry with kitchen paper. Stir into the fromage frais and season to taste.

6 Make the lemon cream sauce: boil the fish trimmings in a little water along with the lemon juice, bay leaf and peppercorns for 10 minutes. Strain into a clean pan and boil rapidly until the liquid has reduced to 150ml/¼ pint, then stir in the cream and season to taste with salt.

Nutrition notes per serving for six: *787 calories, Protein 44g, Carbohydrate 44g, Fat 49g, Saturated fat 10g, Fibre 1g, Added sugar none, Salt 1.56g.*

CRAFTY TIP

Buy a 1.25kg/2¾lb salmon and ask your fishmonger to fillet it and give you the bones and trimmings for the Lemon cream sauce.

SHRIMP GUMBO

Gumbo is a style of cooking that comes from New Orleans and the name of one of the most famous Creole dishes. Gumbos can be made with a variety of ingredients, such as chicken or spiced sausage, as well as shrimp, but my own favourite is this seafood version. Serve piping hot with plenty of plain boiled rice. Gumbo is a style of cooking that comes from New Orleans. It's the Cajun answer to the daubes of France or the stir fries of Canton: a rich, stew-like sauce thickened with either okra or a powdered version of the sassafras root. Gumbos can be made with a variety of ingredients, such as chicken or spiced sausage, as well as shrimp, but my own favourite is a seafood version. You can use ordinary pink cooked prawns to make this dish but it's absolutely outstanding if you can find raw prawns which are blue/black and about the size of a little finger They are usually headless and cook in the sauce enriching it and producing a much finer blend of flavours. Raw prawns are available from many supermarket fish counters as well as from fishmongers. I have even been known to use a mixture of both; raw prawns are quite expensive and one or two per diner with 175g/6oz of conventional prawns lift the sauce and make a good dish. Serve piping hot with plenty of plain boiled rice.

Serves 4

2 tbsp oil

2 onions, chopped

4 celery sticks, sliced

2 red and 2 green peppers, seeded and sliced

225g/8oz okra, cut into 2.5cm/1in pieces

4 ripe tomatoes, skinned and chopped (See Crafty Tip) or 200g can chopped Italian tomatoes

1 tbsp tomato purée

½ tsp freeze-dried thyme

½ tsp chilli powder

salt and freshly ground black pepper

450g/1lb raw prawns, headless and shelled (See Crafty Tip)

chopped fresh parsley, to garnish

1 Heat the oil in a large frying pan. Fry the onions, celery, peppers and okra for about 10 minutes over a medium heat until soft. Add the tomatoes, tomato purée, thyme, chilli powder, seasoning and 250ml/9fl oz water. Bring to the boil and simmer for 30 minutes. Add the prawns for the last 7–10 minutes. Check seasoning and serve garnished with parsley.

Nutrition notes per serving: *239 calories, Protein 25g, Carbohydrate 18g, Fat 8g, Saturated fat 1g, Fibre 7g, Added sugar none, Salt 0.94g.*

CRAFTY TIP

To skin tomatoes: place in a bowl and pour over freshly boiling water to completely cover. Leave to stand: ripe for 30–45 seconds; slightly less ripe for 1 minute and very firm fruit for 1–2 minutes. Any longer and flesh tends to become soft. Drain the tomatoes and slit the skin with the point of a sharp knife, then slide the skin off – it should come away easily in two pieces. Trim at the stalk end if necessary. If you want to remove the seeds, halve the tomatoes and scoop out using a teaspoon.

Vegetarian Dishes

WILD MUSHROOM SALAD Ⓥ

This is equally good made with widely available oyster or champignon mushrooms.

Serves 4

450g/1lb wild mushrooms, washed

4 tbsp olive oil

1 garlic clove, chopped

2 tbsp fresh lemon juice

½ tsp caster sugar

salt and freshly ground black pepper

salad leaves and herbs, to serve

1　Do not peel the mushrooms but slice if they are extra large. Heat half the oil, and cook the mushrooms and garlic for 2 minutes. Mix the lemon juice with the sugar, stirring until the sugar has dissolved.

2　Transfer the mushrooms to a serving bowl and while still warm, toss with the remaining oil and lemon juice. Season, then cool. Make beds of lettuce, radishes and sorrel leaves, top with the mushrooms and sprinkle over the herbs.

Nutrition notes per serving: *125 calories, Protein 3g, Carbohydrate 2g, Fat 12g, Saturated fat 2g, Fibre 1g, Added sugar 1g, Salt 0.39xg.*

VEGETARIAN CASSOULET Ⓥ

I have replaced the meat with vegetables and nuts in this great classic French dish.

Serves 4

450g/1lb dried haricot beans

115g/4oz dried chestnuts

150ml/¼ pint olive oil

4 tbsp thick tomato purée

1 medium onion, studded with cloves

1 garlic clove, crushed

large pinch of freeze-dried oregano

large pinch of freeze-dried thyme

2 bay leaves

½ head of fennel, sliced

225g/8oz button mushrooms

1 large beefsteak tomato, chopped

1 tbsp dark muscovado sugar

1½ tsp salt

freshly ground black pepper

3 tbsp fresh wholemeal breadcrumbs

1　Soak the dried haricot beans for six hours, the dried chestnuts for four hours. Preheat the oven to 350F/180C/Gas 4. Drain the soaked haricot beans, then place in a large pan or flameproof casserole. Add the olive oil, tomato purée, onion, garlic, herbs and bay leaves and cover with water. Bring to the boil for 15 minutes, then transfer to the oven and cook, covered, for 2–2½ hours. You can, if you like, simmer, covered, on top for the same length of time. (It is important not to add any salt at this stage as it affects the cooking of the beans.)

2　Remove the casserole from the heat and discard the onion. Drain the chestnuts and place in the casserole with the fennel, mushrooms, tomato, sugar, salt and pepper to taste. Sprinkle with breadcrumbs and return to the oven for 1 hour.

Nutrition notes per serving: *743 calories, Protein 29g, Carbohydrate 91g, Fat 32g, Saturated fat 4g, Fibre 24g, Added sugar 4g, Salt 1.03g.*

CRAFTY TIP

If you don't like fennel, substitute chopped celery. For extra spiciness you could add a few dashes of Tabasco sauce.

CHEESE FONDUE Ⓥ

Serve this with bread cubes and crispy fresh vegetables

Serves 12–16

350g/12oz Gruyère cheese, grated

350g/12oz Emmental cheese, grated

300ml/½ pint fresh apple juice

1 garlic clove, crushed with salt

1 tbsp cornflour

300ml/½ pint milk

1   In a fondue pan, gently melt the cheeses in the apple juice with the garlic crushed with salt. Whisk the cornflour into the milk and add to the pan when the cheeses start to go runny. Heat gently, stirring, until the sauce thickens and bubbles. Do not overheat.

Nutrition notes per serving for 12: *263 calories, Protein 17g, Carbohydrate 5g, Fat 19g, Saturated fat 12g, Fibre trace, Added sugar none, Salt 1.03g.*

VEGETARIAN COUSCOUS Ⓥ

A traditional vegetarian version from Algeria.

Serves 4–6

175g/6oz chick peas, soaked for 4 hours, drained and boiled for 1 hour

450g/1lb onions, chopped

225g/8oz carrots, chopped

225g/8oz green beans, chopped

225g/8oz courgettes, chopped

225g/8oz tomatoes, chopped

1 garlic clove, crushed

1 tsp turmeric

1 tsp salt

1 tsp freshly ground black pepper

450g/1lb couscous

3 tbsp olive oil

500ml/18fl oz warm water

FOR THE HARISSA

2 garlic cloves

2 tsp chilli powder

½ tsp ground cumin

1   Choose a large pan into which a colander (or sieve) will fit comfortably, leaving at least 15cm/6in underneath. Place the chick peas, vegetables, garlic, turmeric, salt and pepper in the pan. Cover with at least 5cm/2in of water.

2   In a bowl, stir the couscous with the olive oil and 300ml/½ pint of the warm water. The couscous will absorb the water remarkably easily and start to swell up. Keep stirring so it doesn't go lumpy but forms a smooth mixture, then pour into the colander (don't worry it won't fall through the holes).

3   Place the colander in the pan on top of the vegetables and bring the vegetable mixture to the boil over a fairly high heat. Place a tight-fitting lid or tea towel over the top and steam for 30 minutes or until the couscous is thoroughly hot.

4   Remove the couscous from the colander and stir in the remaining warm water, which again will be absorbed. Return couscous to the colander and steam for 10 minutes. (The couscous should now be the size of rice grains.)

5   Place the couscous in a large pile on a serving dish and make a large well in the middle. Drain the vegetables, reserving the stock and place in the well. Moisten the couscous with some of the stock.

6   Make the harissa: mix 225ml/8fl oz of stock with the garlic, chilli powder and cumin in a blender or food processor until smooth and transfer to a bowl.

Nutrition notes per serving for four: *582 calories, Protein 21g, Carbohydrate 100g, Fat 13g, Saturated fat 3g, Fibre 10g, Added sugar none, Salt 1.40g.*

CRAFTY TIP

To eat, take a portion of the couscous, a selection of the vegetables, a pinch of harissa and enough stock to moisten to your taste. Some people like eating it very runny like a soup, others very dry. Either way, it's an amazing combination.

Vegetable Dishes

RED CABBAGE WITH APPLES Ⓥ

This is a vegetarian winter casserole that can be served on its own or with some granary bread. It is great reheated. In Europe, it is traditionally eaten with game such as venison or hare.

Serves 4

450–750g/1–1lb 10oz head red cabbage, cut into 1cm/½in slices

1 large onion, finely chopped

1 cooking apple, cored and finely chopped

2 tbsp oil

2 tsp vinegar

2 tsp (light) muscovado sugar

½ tsp ground cloves

1   Fry the cabbage, onion and apple in the oil over a medium heat, until they glisten. Add 300ml/½ pint of water, the remaining ingredients, then cover and simmer on the lowest heat for at least 40 minutes and preferably 1 hour.

Nutrition notes per serving: *116 calories, Protein 2g, Carbohydrate 14g, Fat 6g, Saturated fat 1g, Fibre 4g, Added sugar 3g, Salt 0.03g.*

CRAFTY TIP

The cabbage loses its bright red, pickled colour and turns a dark, rich purple. It tastes terrific, but don't let it go anywhere near a cream sauce: the combination can be visually disastrous.

CHAMP Ⓥ

This is the Irish version of mashed potatoes. Traditionally, this has melted butter and not fromage frais in the middle. Even more delicious. For the ultimate 'mash' use King Edward, Romano or best of all, Pentland Squire potatoes.

Serves 4

2 tbsp finely chopped spring onions

450g/1lb hot mashed potatoes

4 tbsp fromage frais

freshly ground black pepper

1   Stir the spring onions into the potatoes and arrange the mixture in nests on four plates. Make a well in the middle of each nest and spoon in one tablespoon of fromage frais, then serve sprinkled with freshly ground black pepper.

Nutrition notes per serving: *141 calories, Protein 4g, Carbohydrate 19g, Fat 6g, Saturated fat 4g, Fibre 1g, Added sugar none, Salt 0.25g.*

BRUSSELS SPROUTS POLONAISE ⓥ

Polonaise is a French culinary term used to describe a number of vegetable dishes in which cooked vegetables are covered with a mixture of chopped hard-boiled egg and parsley, then topped with butter-fried breadcrumbs. I often serve this as a vegetable course on its own rather than merely as a subordinate dish to meat or fish.

Serves 4

450g/1lb small Brussels sprouts, trimmed

55g/2oz butter

115g/4oz soft white or wholemeal breadcrumbs

2 hard-boiled eggs (See Crafty Tip), shelled with whites and yolks separated

salt and freshly ground black pepper

1 Plunge the sprouts into boiling water and cook for 7–8 minutes until cooked through but still bright green and firm. Drain, then run a little cold water over to stop them going khaki.

2 In a large frying pan, melt the butter and fry the breadcrumbs over a medium heat until light brown. Add the sprouts, heat through and turn until partially coated with the breadcrumbs. Finely chop the egg whites, add to the pan, check seasoning and spoon into a serving dish. Mash the egg yolks with a fork until crumbly, then sprinkle over and serve.

Nutrition notes per serving: *253 calories, Protein 10g, Carbohydrate 19g, Fat 16g, Saturated fat 8g, Fibre 5g, Added sugar none, Salt 0.99g.*

CRAFTY TIP

To prevent grey yolks and dark rings round the outside of the yolks of hard-boiled eggs, place the eggs in cold water, bring to the boil, then simmer for 10 minutes. Run under cold water, crack the shells and leave until cold before shelling.

CREAMY LAYERED POTATOES (GRATIN DAUPHINOIS) ⓥ

This is one of my and *Food & Drink*'s absolute favourites. Whether or not you are a vegetarian, try this as a main course, perhaps with one or two other vegetables to set it off or just a salad and wholemeal bread.

Serves 4

1 garlic clove, cut in half

750g/1lb 10oz King Edward, Pentland Squire or Cara potatoes, thinly sliced

salt and freshly ground black pepper

55g/2oz butter, plus extra for greasing

150ml/¼ pint double cream

150ml/¼ pint semi-skimmed milk

1 Preheat the oven to 400F/200C/Gas 6. Rub the inside of an earthenware baking dish with the cut sides of the garlic clove and leave to dry, then grease the dish with a little butter. Place a layer of potatoes in the dish, season and spread over a little butter. Repeat layering until all the potatoes have been used.

2 Mix the cream and milk together and pour over the potatoes, then dot with remaining butter. Cook for 30 minutes, then reduce the oven temperature to 350F/180C/Gas 4 and cook for another 30 minutes. The potatoes should be browned on the surface and golden and creamy on the inside.

Nutrition notes per serving: *425 calories, Protein 6g, Carbohydrate 35g, Fat 30g, Saturated fat 19g, Fibre 2g, Added sugar none, Salt 0.63g.*

Desserts

SUSSEX POND PUDDING

There are two versions of this solid suet pudding from south-east England, one from Sussex one from Kent. The only difference seems to be that the Kent one (called Kentish Well Pudding) includes dried fruit, particularly currants, whereas the Sussex one doesn't. Serve with Real egg custard (page 62).

Serves 6

225g/8oz self-raising flour

1 egg

175g/6oz vegetarian suet

FOR THE FILLING

115g/4oz butter, diced

115g/4oz (light) muscovado sugar

115g/4oz currants (for the Kent version)

1 unwaxed lemon

1 By hand, or in a blender or food processor, mix the flour, egg and suet with about 150ml/¼ pint water to make a soft malleable dough. Roll out on a lightly floured board to 5mm/¼in thick. Using two-thirds of the dough, line a 1.2 litre/2 pint pudding basin (See Crafty Tip), reserve the remainder for a lid.

2 Place half the butter, half the sugar and half the currants, if you are using them, in the basin. Then, using a sharp, thin instrument (a hat pin is ideal), pierce the lemon all over and stand in the bowl on the filling. Top with remaining filling ingredients so that the lemon is covered. Cover with the pastry lid and seal firmly round the edges.

3 Cover the basin in buttered foil, pleated, to allow for steam expansion during cooking. Tie with enough string to leave a handle on top for easy removal, then steam for 3 hours in a pan, or for 1 hour in a pressure cooker.

4 Remove the foil from the basin and turn out pudding by placing a serving bowl over the basin and turning both upside down together. Make a cut in the pastry so that the juices flow out, forming a 'pond'.

Nutrition notes per serving: *615 calories, Protein 5g, Carbohydrate 49g, Fat 46g, Saturated fat 18g, Fibre 1g, Added sugar 20g, Salt 0.74g.*

CRAFTY TIP

To line the bowl with suet pastry: roll out the dough into a circle about 10cm/4in larger than the top of the basin. Cut a quarter segment out for the lid. Dust the top of the three-quarter section with a little flour, then fold in half so that the cut edges lie on top of each other. Lift the folded dough into the basin, then open out and press around the sides to completely line the basin. Brush the cut edges with a little water and overlap slightly to seal the join.

BLACKBERRY COBBLER Ⓕ

Fruit cobblers are an ancient country tradition in Britain and a frugal one: a hot, baked pudding with a topping made from stale bread. The cut-up bread, waiting to be used and lying in rows like the leather heels in a cobbler's shop, gave the dish its name. You can vary the fruits used for this pudding according to the time of year. Try rhubarb and ginger, plums, cherries or apples when in season. Serve with Real egg custard (page 62).

Serves 4-6

450g/1lb blackberries, thawed if frozen (See Crafty Tip)

140g/5oz caster sugar

1 small bloomer loaf

1 egg

150ml/¼ pint milk

pinch of ground allspice

½ tsp freshly grated nutmeg

1 Preheat the oven to 350F/180C/Gas 4. Place the blackberries in a 850ml/1½ pint pie dish and mix with 115g/4oz of sugar. Cut the loaf in half lengthways, then cut one of the halves into 1cm/½in slices to make the 'cobbles'.

2 Beat the egg and milk with the allspice and dip the bread pieces in the mixture. Place over the top of the blackberries, overlapping, to form a 'cobbled' effect. Sprinkle with the remaining sugar and the nutmeg, then bake for 20 minutes until golden.

Nutrition notes per serving for four: *365 calories, Protein 9g, Carbohydrate 76g, Fat 5g, Saturated fat 1g, Fibre 4g, Added sugar 37g, Salt 0.95g.*

CRAFTY TIP

Blackberries are native to Britain, Europe and other temperate zones. They grow wild in woodlands and hedgerows from late July until the first frosts. Wild blackberries are small and firm with a delicious sweet, yet tart flavour and rather more seed than flesh. Cultivated blackberries tend to be larger, plumper and juicier and taste almost as good. If out picking your own, avoid fruit near a road or in a field that may have been sprayed. The fruit should be eaten as soon as possible after picking or buying but if you do need to store, hull (pull out any remaining stalk and the pithy hull will follow) and keep in the fridge for up to two days. Rinse in a colander just before using. When buying, choose blackberries that are firm, dry and purple-black with no green or red patches and no signs of mould. Steer clear of punnets with fruit-stained bases – it's a sure sign of squashed fruit.

✳ Dry blackberries can be frozen whole, but moist samples should be made into a pulp or purée before freezing. Open freeze on trays until firm, then transfer to freezing bags and store for up to 1 year.

BREAD AND BUTTER PUDDING

This is now the most popular restaurant pudding in Britain. It can be eaten hot or cold. I prefer it warm with just a little pouring cream to add a touch of moisture and richness.

Serves 4

55g/2oz butter, softened, plus extra for greasing

4 x 2.5cm/1in thick slices fresh white bread

25g/1oz raisins

25g/1oz sultanas

25g/1oz chopped candied peel

55g/2oz caster sugar

2 eggs

300ml/½ pint milk

½ tsp freshly grated nutmeg

1 Preheat the oven to 350F/180C/Gas 4. Lightly butter a baking dish about 15cm/6in across and at least 5–7.5cm/2–3in deep.

2 Butter the bread, cutting off any hard crusts. Cut into four fingers per slice. Place a layer of bread in the dish, sprinkle over some raisins, sultanas, candied peel and sugar and repeat layering, making three or four layers altogether. Beat the eggs and milk together, then pour over the bread through a sieve. The liquid should just come to below the very top of the bread. Gently press the bread under the liquid with a spoon. If you need to, add a little more milk to bring it up to this level, then sprinkle with nutmeg.

3 Place the dish in a bain-marie, that is a baking dish filled with 2.5cm/1in of water and bake for 35–40 minutes until the custard is set and the top is golden brown but not in any way burnt.

Nutrition notes per serving: *396 calories, Protein 10g, Carbohydrate 52g, Fat 18g, Saturated fat 10g, Fibre 1g, Added sugar 18g, Salt 1.09g.*

TREACLE TART

This is an adaptation of a traditional English recipe – the walnuts add a little crunch. It is best eaten warm with lots of pouring cream or Real egg custard (page 62).

Serves 4-6

1 quantity of Shortcrust pastry (page 62)

115g/4oz butter, softened

55g/2oz caster sugar

2 eggs, beaten

175g/6oz golden syrup or 115g/4oz golden syrup and 55g/2oz treacle

115g/4oz walnuts, finely chopped

grated rind of 1 lemon

juice of ½ lemon

pinch of salt

1 Preheat the oven to 400F/200C/Gas 6. Roll out the pastry and use to line a 20cm/8in tin with straight sides. Cover the base with crumpled kitchen foil to stop it bubbling in the middle and bake for 10 minutes. Turn the oven temperature down to 350F/180C/Gas 4 when you remove the pastry case.

2 Mix together the butter and sugar until smooth, then beat in the eggs and syrup (warm the syrup gently in a pan if it's too cold to pour). Add the walnuts, the grated rind and lemon juice and the salt. Remove the foil in the pastry case and spoon in the treacle mixture, then bake for 45–55 minutes until the top is brown and crispy.

Nutrition notes per serving for four: *1050 calories, Protein 13g, Carbohydrate 98g, Fat 70g, Saturated fat 33g, Fibre 3g, Added sugar 53g, Salt 2.36g.*

CRAFTY TIP

This tart is not improved by keeping in the fridge, the filling tends to collapse a bit and the pastry goes soggy.

RASPBERRY FOOL

A deliciously easy and refreshing 18th-century dessert. Try in June with fresh raspberries.

Serves 4

225g/8oz raspberries, thawed if frozen

55g/2oz caster sugar

150ml/¼ pint double cream

140g/5oz natural yogurt

fresh mint leaves and whole raspberries, to decorate

1   Crush the raspberries with a fork and mix with the sugar and set aside. Whisk the double cream until it is peaking, then beat in the yogurt a spoonful at a time. Stir the raspberries into the cream to achieve a marbled effect. Transfer to four wine glasses, chill for 30 minutes, then decorate and serve.

Nutrition notes per serving: *255 calories, Protein 3g, Carbohydrate 20g, Fat 19g, Saturated fat 12g, Fibre 1g, Added sugar 14g, Salt 0.11g.*

CRAFTY CRÊPES SUZETTE ✸

This was originally a very complicated and grand recipe that began with grating orange and lemon rinds and finished with a dramatic piece of flambéing.

Serves 4

55g/2oz butter

125ml/4fl oz fresh orange juice

2 tbsp orange and lemon marmalade

grated rind of 1 lemon

1–2 tbsp brandy or rum (optional)

FOR THE CREPES

115g/4oz fine plain flour

pinch of salt

1 egg, beaten

½ tbsp oil (not olive)

175ml/6fl oz fresh orange juice

1   Make the crêpes: mix the flour, salt, egg and oil together, then add the orange juice. Whisk thoroughly until smooth, then rest for 30 minutes in the fridge. Up to 1½ hours won't hurt. Very lightly grease a heavy 25cm/10in frying pan, pour in a generous tablespoon of batter and swirl it round, covering as much area as you can. It will set and go curly at the edges and may be so thin that there are even a few holes. Do not panic. Leave for 30–45 seconds, turn over, cook for 30–45 seconds, then place on a warm plate. Cook the remaining seven crepes the same way. Stack, separated by greaseproof paper.

2   Make the sauce: in a 30cm/12in frying pan, melt the butter until it foams, add the orange juice and marmalade and stir until the mixture melts together. Sprinkle on the lemon rind and add the crêpes, one by one, making sure they are coated in the sauce. Fold them into quarters and pile on one side of the pan as you go.

3   If you feel like risking your eyebrows flambé with the brandy, making sure all the alcohol is burnt off. Or simply serve two pancakes to each person, with a good spoonful of orange sauce.

Nutrition notes per serving: *298 calories, Protein 5g, Carbohydrate 35g, Fat 14g, Saturated fat 8g, Fibre 1g, Added sugar 7g, Salt 0.56g.*

CRAFTY TIP

✸ Make double and freeze any left-over. Interleave with non-stick baking parchment, and pack in a large polythene bag or foil. They can be frozen for 3 months. Separate by sliding a palette knife between them. Defrost a large stack in the fridge overnight. Individual crêpes thaw quickly at room temperature.

Basic Recipes

REAL EGG CUSTARD

This is the original version of that great British favourite, custard. It is slightly paler and less sweet than powdered custards but infinitely more delicious.

Serves 4–6

3 egg yolks

2 dessertspoons caster sugar

1 tsp cornflour

1 tsp vanilla essence

300ml/½ pint milk

1   Whisk together the egg yolks, sugar, cornflour and vanilla essence. Gently heat the milk to boiling point, then add to the other ingredients. Whisk and return to the pan, simmer gently, stirring continuously until thickened.

CRAFTY TIP

Whisk up remaining egg whites with 175g/6oz caster sugar to make meringues. Or freeze whites in a rigid container for up to a year, labelled with the number of whites.

SHORTCRUST PASTRY

I make all my pastry in a food processor, not least because I have hot hands. It is also much easier to make it this way. You can make it by hand, if you are a purist. This pastry is suitable for sweet and savoury dishes.

Makes enough to line a 20cm/8in flan tin

225g/8oz plain flour

1 tbsp icing sugar

½ tsp salt

115g/4oz butter or white vegetable fat or 55g/2oz of each, softened and diced

1   Place the flour, sugar, salt and fat in a food processor. Process for 10 seconds or until mixture resembles fine breadcrumbs. Add two to three tablespoons of water, one tablespoon at a time, and stop processing as soon as the dough forms a ball round the blade. (Different flours absorb water at different speeds.) Remove dough, press together, wrap in plastic film and chill for 30 minutes.

2   By hand, rub fat into the flour, sugar and salt until mixture resembles fine breadcrumbs, gradually add water until dough clings firmly, wrap and chill.

CRAFTY SAVOURY WHITE SAUCE

Simply add extra ingredients such as cheese, anchovies or mustard to make a sauce to complement fish, meat, vegetable and egg dishes.

Makes 300ml/½ pint

300ml/½ pint milk

25g/1oz butter

25g/1oz plain flour

salt and freshly ground black pepper

1   Whisk the milk, butter and flour together in a pan over a medium heat until it comes to the boil and thickens, then season. Make sure you are whisking at the moment it does come to the boil and you will have a perfectly smooth glossy base sauce.

INDEX